THE
EVERYDAY
GOSPEL

A theology of washing the dishes

Tim Chester

CONTENTS

The Everyday Gospel © 10Publishing 2013 Tim Chester

Published in 2013 by 10Publishing, a division of 10ofthose.com
9D Centurion Court, Farington, Leyland PR25 3UQ, England.

Email: info@10ofthose.com Website: www.10ofthose.com

ISBN 978-1-909611-16-0

Design by Mike Thorpe / www.design-chapel.com

Printed by CPI Group (UK) Ltd, Croydon, CR0 4YY

THE UNHAPPY LEGALIST

How do you know a legalist has washed the dishes?

It might sound like the first half of a joke. But I am serious.

You might not consider washing the dishes one of the pressing issues facing the church today. But it is one most Christians face two or three times a day. How should the gospel inform our washing of the dishes? What does a theology of it look like? What is holy washing of dishes? How can we consecrate this work?

The point, of course, is not that washing the dishes is more important than other things. Rather, it represents countless ordinary activities we do each day. How does the gospel shape our attitude and approach to everyday life? Is Christian faith for Monday as well as Sunday mornings?

So let us come back to our opening question. How do you know a legalist has washed the dishes?

The answer is: They wash up most of the cutlery and crockery, but they leave the pans 'to soak' and they do not wipe down the kitchen surfaces. I am a great advocate of soaking, but it can be used as an excuse to leave the job unfinished.

Why is this? Because they are not doing it out of a love for God and others. They are doing it because they feel they ought to, or because they want to be seen to be doing it. So there's no intrinsic joy in it.

The legalist says, 'I do this because I ought to do it, even though I don't want to do it.' The key word is 'ought' – that is the motivation. Because they do not really want to do it, they do just enough to claim it is done.

The gospel says, 'I do this because I want to.'

In the case of washing the dishes, they do just enough to be able to say they have done it. Most of the washing is done, but the kitchen is not left clean.

That is why legalists like rules. Rules define your obligation tightly, so you can know when you have done enough.

That is the motivation of the teacher of the law who asks in Luke 10, 'Who is my neighbour?' Luke tells us, '. . . he wanted to justify himself, so he asked Jesus, "And who is my neighbour?"' (Luke 10:29). Jesus tells him he needs to love God and love his neighbour to inherit eternal life. So he wants to know when the task of loving his neighbour is complete. He wants to end the day by being able to say, 'Love for God. Tick. Love for neighbour. Tick. Done. Finished.'

'Washing the dishes? No dirty dishes. Tick. Done. Finished. Justified.'

The problem for this unhappy legalist is that Jesus tells the story of the Good Samaritan which completely explodes all his categories of love for neighbour, making it an impossible task which cannot be ticked off a list.

If legalism says, 'I do this because I ought to do it even though I don't want to', then what does the gospel say? The gospel says, 'I do this because I want to.' The Holy Spirit gives us new desires, a new motivation. We want to do what is right, we want to love God, we want to love others. We find joy in doing the right thing because it is the right thing.

That does not mean it is not tough. Often the joy is perceived only by faith. We are called to deny ourselves and take up our cross. Life may not often be fun. But we

> That does not mean it is not tough. Often the joy is perceived only by faith. We are called to deny ourselves and take up our cross.

can find joy in doing the right thing, in bringing glory to God and loving other people. No one will find joy in the act of being persecuted, for example, but we can rejoice, as the apostles did in Acts 5:41, that we have been counted worthy of suffering disgrace for the name of Jesus.

But I think we can go a bit further when it comes to washing the dishes.

How do we find joy in it?

WASHING THE DISHES IS A GOD-LIKE ACTIVITY
#1: Ordering Chaos

First, we can share the joy of the Creator as we bring order from chaos. Genesis 1:1–5 says:

In the beginning God created the heavens and the earth. Now the earth was formless and empty, darkness was over the surface of the deep, and the Spirit of God was hovering over the waters.

And God said, 'Let there be light,' and there was light. God saw that the light was good, and he separated the light from the darkness. God called the light 'day', and the darkness he called 'night'. And there was evening, and there was morning – the first day.

God's first creative act was to bring order from chaos.

And that first creative act is prototypical for all creative acts. Being made in the image of the Creator to care for his creation means we are made to share his joy in order and beauty. We sweep a yard and then lean on the broom handle admiring what we have done. That is a profound act. We are expressing our true humanity and sharing in God's joy at creation. It is the same with washing the dishes. The dirty dishes become a pile of clean crockery. The cluttered kitchen becomes new again.

Notice the structure of the creation account in Genesis 1. Verse 2 says the earth was 'formless and empty'. It seems the creation account is structured to present God's creative activity as the antidote to this primordial chaos. In days one to three God takes what was formless and gives it form. And then in days four to six God takes what is empty and fills it. And the second three days match the first three days. On day one God creates light and dark, and on day four he creates the sun, moon and stars to fill the heavens. On day two God creates water and sky, and on day five he fills the waters with fish and the skies with birds. On day three God creates land, and on day six he fills the land with animals.

So God orders and he fills. He orders the chaos on days one to three and he fills the emptiness on days four to six.

Notice, too, what God's work of ordering involves. It involves two things: separating and naming. Separating and naming are activities that God only does on days one to three. God separates light and dark, he separates sky and sea, he separates sea and land. And he names the light 'day' and the darkness 'night'. He names the expanse above 'sky'. He names the dry ground 'land' and the waters 'seas'.

God brings form out of what was formless. He brings order out of chaos.

Separating and naming. Tidying and labelling. God brings form out of what was formless. He brings order out of chaos. He tidies up creation.

And when he looks at what he has done he sees that it is good. It is good to bring order out of chaos. It is good to tidy up. It is good to label up.

Perhaps you are one of those people who like to write beautiful handwritten sticky labels. People will tell you that you are just being anally retentive. Do not believe it – it is a divine activity! The pleasure that there is in these activities is an echo of the pleasure of God on the first days of creation.

Notice, too, the task that is given to humanity. Look at Genesis 1:28:

God blessed them and said to them, 'Be fruitful and increase in number; fill the earth and subdue it. Rule over the fish of the sea and the birds of the air and over every living creature that moves on the ground.'

It is a two-fold task: to govern or rule and to fill or be fruitful. Ring any bells? Humanity made in God's image is given a task that mirrors God's own creative activity. We are to govern. We are to bring order where there is chaos,

We are to bring order where there is chaos, form to what is formless.

form to what is formless – just as God did on days one to three. And then we are to fill – just as God did on days four to six.

What does Adam's governing activity look like in Genesis 2? Naming the animals. What did God's governing activity look like on days one to three? *Separating and naming.* On days one, two and three God does the naming (day, night, sky, land, seas). On days four, five and six no naming takes place. Naming the inhabitants of days four to six is given to humanity. The task of naming is begun by God, but extended to us.

The divine activity of governing chaos, ordering what is formless, bringing beauty out of mess, tidying up creation – that task is given to humanity made in God's image. And it is good!

When you have done the dishes, tidied everything away, wiped down the surfaces and look round the kitchen with pleasure – that is a divine feeling.

When I was reading Genesis 1 with a friend who was born and brought up in Rotherham, we paraphrased the 'it was good' with the words, 'Job's a good 'un.'

It is a good job. A job well done. Job's a good 'un. That's a divine pleasure.

WASHING THE DISHES IS A GOD-LIKE ACTIVITY
#2: Serving Others

Second, we can enjoy the opportunity to serve others. If in our home we have left the dirty dishes from the night before, I love doing it in the morning while my wife is still in bed. I love the thought of her coming down thinking of the work that needs doing to find the kitchen all clean!

Sin is living for self instead of living for God – running my life my way. But this autonomy does not lead to freedom or joy. I am not functioning in the manner for which I was created. I have redefined my purpose. That means I have now become the wrong tool for the job. I am not designed for autonomy. It is like cutting a hedge with a pencil. It just creates frustration. A person turned in on themselves becomes a lesser person. So many of our psychological problems stem from this inversion and introversion. We were not made to look inward for self-realization, but to look outwards in love.

I am made in the image of the triune God, the God who said, 'Let *us* make man in *our* image' (Gen. 1:26, my italics). God is persons-in-relationship. And we are made in his image. Humanity is persons-in-relationship. I find my identity in relationships, not in autonomy: Tim Chester is the son of Richard and Judith, the husband of Helen, the father of Katie and Hannah, a member of a specific Christian community and a child of God. No one else is that combination of relationships. This is what gives me my identity. This is what makes me unique. But this identity is intrinsically relational. I find myself in relationships, in service, in love, in washing the dishes.

> I find myself in relationships, in service, in love, in washing the dishes.

Moreover, when my autonomous self meets another autonomous person there is conflict. We are both committed to living our own way, and something has to give. So we live in a world of conflict, resentment, oppression. And that is often played out at the kitchen sink. The kitchen sink can become a place of tyranny or resentment.

At this point and in this place Jesus calls us to deny ourselves, to take up our cross and follow him. He calls us to a way of life defined by the cross. Martyrdom begins at the kitchen sink. Every time you embrace washing the dishes you are dying to self. It is an act of martyrdom in miniature.

How do we move from washing the dishes as an unpleasant duty to joyful service? From resentment to rejoicing? Part of the answer is, I think, to offer the washing of dishes to God as an act of service, to consciously think of doing the dishes in God's presence for God's pleasure. Hebrews 13:15,16 says:

> *Through Jesus, therefore, let us continually offer to God a sacrifice of praise – the fruit of lips that confess his name. And do not forget to do good and to share with others, for with such sacrifices God is pleased.*

As priests of the New Covenant we continually offer God sacrifices. The word 'continually' is surely a surprise to the reader of Hebrews! 'Let us *continually* offer to God a sacrifice.' The great central section of Hebrews has as its point and climax the declaration that Jesus has offered one complete, finished sacrifice for sins:

'Let us *continually* offer to God a sacrifice.'

> *Day after day every priest stands and performs his religious duties; again and again he offers the same sacrifices, which can never take away sins. But when*

this priest had offered for all time one sacrifice for sins,
he sat down at the right hand of God. (Heb. 10:11,12)

The job was done. Old Covenant sacrifices were continual, but the New Covenant sacrifice of Jesus is complete.

The key thing is that this is not a sacrifice of atonement, but a sacrifice of praise.

Now we are told 'continually' to offer to God a sacrifice. The key thing is that this is not a sacrifice of atonement, but a sacrifice of praise. It is offered 'through Jesus' not instead of, or to supplement, the sacrifice of Jesus. We respond to the finished work of Christ with a continual sacrifice of praise, worship, love, gratitude, affection and joy.

Notice what form this takes. It is the fruit of lips that confess his name. It is sung and said. But it is also doing good and sharing with others. It is also lived and loved. It is also washing the dishes. Doing the dishes is a sacrifice of praise for the finished sacrifice of Christ.

When I wash up I deny myself. I put others first. I say, in effect, that someone matters more to me than my comfort. And that someone is Jesus. When I was living for self I would gladly let others do the dishes. But now Jesus is my treasure, my life, my joy. And so offering him a sacrifice of washing the dishes becomes my delight. To offer the washing to him as a sacrifice of praise points my heart back to the cross, back to the place where I find love, mercy and grace. It points me back to the place where my heart is melted and moulded.

I recently reread *The Practice of the Presence of God* by Brother Lawrence, the seventeenth-century monk who famously found that an awareness of God's presence with him transformed his kitchen duties from a burden to a joy. I have to say I was pleasantly surprised by what I found. This is what he said (I have updated the archaic language):

Sanctification does not involve changing what we do, but in doing our normal activities for God's sake.

At first developing the habit of having a continual conversation with God and referring all that we do to him requires discipline. But after a while God's love motivates us to do it without difficulty.

When I became distracted, God would remind me of some truth that I found so exciting that I could not contain myself. I was more united to God in my everyday activities than in my formal devotions. There is no special technique for going to God, just a heart determined to apply itself to nothing but God.

We ought not to get tired of doing little things for God because God does not look at the greatness of our

> Sanctification does not involve changing what we do, but in doing our normal activities for God's sake.

activities, but the love with which they are performed. At first doing everything for God will be hard, but it can become a habit. That's because the more we do everything for God, the more we will find delight in doing everything for him.

There is no special technique for going to God, just a heart determined to apply itself to nothing but God.

It is a remarkable grace-filled book. There will be times when you wash the dishes with a resentful heart. What do you do then? Brother Lawrence's chronicler says:

Brother Lawrence was well aware of his faults, but not discouraged by them. He simply confessed them to God without making any excuses. And then returned in peace to his usual practice of adoring and loving God . . . He placed his sins between him and God to show that he did not deserve God's favours. But God still continued to bless him abundantly.

The link between serving and leading means that washing the dishes is also a great testing and training ground for leadership. I would be reluctant to recognize as a leader someone who was not quick to wash up. Indeed I have not appointed people for that very reason. I am not looking for leaders who are good at washing the dishes, but a reluctance to serve others by washing the dishes suggests someone who wants to be a leader for their own glory, not to serve others through the Word. Jesus famously said to his disciples:

> You know that those who are regarded as rulers of the Gentiles lord it over them, and their high officials exercise authority over them. Not so with you. Instead, whoever wants to become great among you must be your servant, and whoever wants to be first must be slave of all. For even the Son of Man did not come to be served, but to serve, and to give his life as a ransom for many. (Mark 10:42–45)

A true leader is one who serves. Leadership is not about who does what at the front in the limelight. It begins with serving one another.

In 1 Timothy 3 Paul says he writes so that people will know how to 'conduct themselves in God's household' (v. 15), or God's family. The church is a household or family. So when Paul outlines the requirements of a leader in 1 Timothy 3, he says:

> He must manage his own family well and see that his children obey him with proper respect. (If anyone does not know how to manage his own family, how can he take care of God's church?) (vv. 4,5)

In other words, the way a man behaves in his household is a good indication of the way he will behave in the church. If he lords it over his household, then he is likely to lord it over the church. If he washes up in the home, then he is likely to serve within the church. If he always needs to be asked to do the dishes in the home, then he is unlikely to take the initiative within the church, unlikely to take responsibility for what is happening, unlikely to be proactive in serving others. This is why washing the dishes is a great testing and training ground for leadership.

If he always needs to be asked to do the dishes in the home, then he is unlikely to take the initiative within the church.

To recap: There are two reasons for finding joy in washing the dishes. First, we share the pleasure of God in creation as we bring order out of chaos. Second, we turn from self-centredness to be the other-centred people we were made to be as we serve God and others.

WHEN WASHING THE DISHES GOES BAD

However, these two reasons can be perverted. Washing the dishes can go bad – 'dirty' washing the dishes, if you like.

Our first reason for finding joy in washing the dishes is sharing the joy of the Creator in bringing order to chaos. But sometimes the desire to bring order becomes excessive. Cleaning becomes an obsession. We can become fixated on ordering our kitchen in a particular way. Our kitchen becomes our domain. In this world of chaos and threat, here is a little bit of space in which I am sovereign. We shoo others out of 'our' kitchen. 'It'll be easier if I do it myself.' 'You wouldn't do it right.' Or we enforce perfection. We get annoyed when people put things away in the wrong place. Think about the word 'wrong' in the phrase 'the wrong place'. Who determines right and wrong in this situation? Not the living God.

The issue is not defining what is excessive cleanliness (How clean is clean?). The problem is the desire for order is no longer a governing of God's world, but a governing of my world. It is no longer a governing of the world for glory of God and the good of other people. Governing has become an end in itself. I want to be my own lord.

The second perversion is the perversion of service. This can take a number of forms, but what they have in common is a desire to be my own saviour.

We have already identified the legalist who does the minimum required but no more. They may want to be able to think of themselves as a good person who has helped others, or they may want to impress people so others think well of them, or they may want to prove themselves to God. Whichever it is, they are trying to be their own saviour.

Sometimes this self-justification means we do the minimum we can get away with. At other times, it may express itself in a martyr complex.

Sometimes this self-justification means we do the minimum we can get away with. At other times, it may express itself in a martyr complex. We have already said that washing the dishes is rightly martyrdom in miniature; a dying to self through which we find ourselves. But this can be perverted into a martyr complex: 'No, I'll do it. You go off and enjoy yourself. Leave it to me, I'm OK.' We present ourselves (often somewhat resentfully) as suffering on behalf of others. We do the washing the dishes so they can have a good time. Now we are not only our own saviour, but also the saviour of others. We bear not only our sins, but the sins of the world!

WHEN YOU SHOULD NOT WASH UP

I think gospel reflection on doing the dishes also means we can identify some times when it is not right to wash up; when we should let others do it.

To show you why, let me ask you a question. Men who rarely do the cooking in the kitchen often take charge of the BBQ. Why is that? It might be something to do with pyromaniac tendencies in men, but I suspect it is also because many men are unsure of what to do in social situations. They feel uncomfortable standing around making small talk so they congregate around the BBQ, discussing how well it is going.

Something similar, I think, can happen with washing the dishes. Doing the dishes can function as an escape from social interactions. So sometimes we need to *not* wash up, so we can serve others by talking with them, making them feel welcome, encouraging them with the gospel.

Or here is another situation when we should not do the dishes. The kitchen sink is a great training ground. It is a place where we learn to serve. So it is important to encourage our children to wash up. And by 'encourage' I mean 'make'.

The kitchen sink is a great training ground. It is a place where we learn to serve. So it is important to encourage our children to wash up.

But here is the problem. That is often hard work – harder than doing it yourself. They moan. There is a fight. They do a bad job. You have to do some of it again. They leave all the difficult stuff. They make a mess on the floor. And on top of all that, they resent you for the rest of the evening. It just feels easier to do it yourself.

However, the aim of your interaction with your children is surely not an easy life. What *are* your aims?

- To teach them life skills so they can transition into adulthood. Washing the dishes is a basic life-skill.

- To teach them to serve others. So do not bribe them to wash up. Teach them to serve because serving is the right thing to do. Service is to be its own reward.

- To teach them justice and grace. Allocate responsibilities with as much fairness as you can because you want to model justice. But also encourage them to serve without looking to a direct quid pro quo.

Our ultimate aim is to teach our children to live under loving authority. God has given parents to children so they can learn the freedom of living this way (Eph. 6:1–4). The family is a training ground for a life lived under various spheres of authority (teachers, police, employers). Even more importantly, the family is a mirror of the loving authority of our heavenly Father. Getting your children to wash up is a gospel opportunity, a chance to teach them that freedom is not rejecting God's authority, but living under the liberating, loving, life-giving rule of God.

Our ultimate aim is to teach our children to live under loving authority.

On the subject of not doing the washing the dishes, what about guests?

Let me suggest two principles:

- Not letting someone do the dishes is a sign of honour.

- Inviting someone to do the dishes is a sign of inclusion.

In other words, washing the dishes is both a marker of a guest and a marker of family. So there can be no universal principle which determines whether guests are invited or allowed to wash up. Sometimes you may want to prevent your guests from washing- up as a sign of honour;

sometimes you may invite them to wash up as a sign of inclusion.

You may want to treat the same person differently on different occasions. There may be times when you treat people to a fancy meal, and wash up when they have gone. There may be other times when they share your life as a family, and wash up with you.

Washing up is a great opportunity for discipleship and pastoral care. It is, first of all, an opportunity to learn how to serve. It is a way of training people not to think of themselves, but to think of others. Paul says to thieves:

> *He who has been stealing must steal no longer, but must work, doing something useful with his own hands, that he may have something to share with those in need. (Eph. 4:28)*

A thief is renewed not when he stops stealing, but when he gives to the poor. More than that, he is renewed through the act of giving to the poor, by reorienting their lives away from self towards others. And doing the dishes can perform the same function for self-centred, self-absorbed or selfish people.

A thief is renewed not when they stop stealing, but when they give to the poor.

Washing the dishes is also an activity that allows for challenging conversations. Consider what it is like sitting opposite someone as you challenge their behaviour or explore personal issues that touch upon deep hurts. It is likely to be an intense encounter. They are eye-to-eye. Sometimes that is important, but it can be threatening. Silences are likely to be poignant. But washing the dishes (like sharing other chores, or a journey) allows for a natural mix of eye contact and non-eye contact, for conversation and natural silences. The activity means the encounter is less intense. So washing the dishes is a great context for pastoral care.

EVERYDAY LIFE AS DIVINE REVELATION

In Romans 1:18–23 Paul says:

The wrath of God is being revealed from heaven against all the godlessness and wickedness of men who suppress the truth by their wickedness, since what may be known about God is plain to them, because God has made it plain to them. For since the creation of the world God's invisible qualities – his eternal power and divine nature – have been clearly seen, being understood from what has been made, so that men are without excuse.

For although they knew God, they neither glorified him as God nor gave thanks to him, but their thinking became futile and their foolish hearts were darkened. Although they claimed to be wise, they became fools and exchanged the glory of the immortal God for images made to look like mortal man and birds and animals and reptiles

'...what may be known about God is plain to them...God's invisible qualities ... have been clearly seen' (vv. 19,20). The world is a revelation of God. This encompasses both nature and history. This is known as natural theology and has been used in apologetics. People have tried to prove God from the world around us or pointed to the beauty of the world as a testimony to God. The problem is that 'men ...suppress the truth by their wickedness' (v. 18) Humanity knew God through creation, but 'they neither glorified him as God nor gave thanks to him' and so, as a result, 'their thinking became futile and their foolish hearts were darkened' (v. 21). The revelation of creation is distorted, warped, rejected because humanity will not know God.

The image Paul creates here is of the revelation of God pressing down on humanity and humanity pushing it away. This is not an event. It is a constant process. God's revelation is constantly pressing down on humanity and humanity is constantly pushing it away.

God's revelation is constantly pressing down on humanity and humanity is constantly pushing it away.

It is not that we *cannot* believe, but that we *will* not. The truth is out there, but we push it away. The problem is not with our heads, but with our hearts. We will not believe what we do not want to live. People reject the knowledge of God because they do not want to live with the implications. They do not want to glorify him nor give him thanks. They do not want to live in submission to God, nor in dependence on him.

The result is that the value of natural theology for apologetics is limited. We cannot demonstrate God from creation not because the revelation is not there, but because people suppress that revelation. This is not to say it has no value. It helps us show that people's objections, however rational they may appear, reflect the rejection of God in their hearts. And natural theology is also helpful for those who are genuinely seeking after God.

Even if natural theology is of limited value in apologetics, we must not miss the fact that the revelation of God is there in nature and history. Those with the Spirit now have eyes to see it. We have the Word of God to reorient us to creation.

This is what many of the psalms are doing. Consider, for example, Psalm 104:24–30:

> *How many are your works, O Lord!*
>
> > *In wisdom you made them all;*
> >
> > *the earth is full of your creatures.*
>
> *There is the sea, vast and spacious,*
>
> > *teeming with creatures beyond number –*

living things both large and small.

There the ships go to and fro,

    and the leviathan, which you formed to frolic there.

These all look to you

    to give them their food at the proper time.

When you give it to them,

    they gather it up;

when you open your hand,

    they are satisfied with good things.

When you hide your face,

    they are terrified;

when you take away their breath,

    they die and return to the dust.

When you send your Spirit,

    they are created,

    and you renew the face of the earth.

Psalm 104 is an invitation to see in creation a revelation of God (see also Ps. 65). We see in creation a Creator of vast variety, a Creator who provides for his creation, a Creator upon whom we depend for life.

Or consider Psalm 93:3,4:

The seas have lifted up, O LORD,

the seas have lifted up their voice;

the seas have lifted up their pounding waves.

Mightier than the thunder of the great waters,

mightier than the breakers of the sea –

the LORD on high is mighty.

We experience the sea as a mighty force, and this points to the greater might of its Creator.

Or consider Job 38 to 41 where God himself invites Job to ponder the world around him. Creation is beyond our understanding and beyond our control. And the ways of God are likewise beyond our understanding and control.

What this means is that everyday life is a revelation of God.

As I do the dishes, I look out of my window and see the sparrows. I marvel at the beauty of God's creation and remember his care. This was the theme of Psalm 104 and this is the natural theology of Jesus in Luke 12: 'Are not five sparrows sold for two pennies? Yet not one of them is forgotten by God. Indeed, the very hairs of your head are all numbered. Don't be afraid; you are worth more than many sparrows' (vv. 6,7). My heavenly Father knows each one, remembers each one, cares for each one. And so I need not be afraid, because I am worth more than mere birds.

I can know the care of God through what I observe in the natural world.But it is not just the natural world. I could reflect on the technology of dishwashing liquid. Human beings have created this substance that readily breaks down grease and grime while leaving my hands lovely and soft! Or I listen to music on the radio; beautiful sounds that not only delight me, but connect me with other listeners in a shared experience, one which is again mediated through technology. Here I discern the creativity of the Creator, along with the gift of freedom that he gives to human beings – the invitation to take his creation and refashion it in new ways that (at best) foster human community and bring God glory.

I can know the care of God through what I observe in the natural world.But it is not just the natural world. I could reflect on the technology of dishwashing liquid.

Or consider the remnants of the meal that I am wiping from the plate or the leftovers that I am picking over. Here is fuel for my body, but which (most of the time) is something that brings delight. My body is not sustained by being plugged into a socket. It is sustained by meals that taste good and which come in a myriad of forms. It reminds me of the abundant generosity of the Creator. He is not utilitarian. He is constantly going beyond what is required to express his joy, his glory, his abundance, his beauty.

This spaghetti carbonara locates me within a tradition of Italian cooking, the fruit of which I now share. It reminds me that we not only have human creativity, but we have traditions of human creativity. We have cultures and heritages which one day will be part of the new creation as the kings of the world bring their glory into the new Jerusalem (Rev. 21:24,26).

We have cultures and heritages which one day will be part of the new creation as the kings of the world bring their glory.

It reminds me, too, that human identity and creativity is relational. My spaghetti carbonara is part of a tradition of Italian cooking, but it is also unique. It is both continuous with other carbonaras, and discontinuous. I express my creative activity in the relational context of a shared heritage. My identity is found in relationship to, rather than distinction from, my context, but in a way that does not force me into conformity.

There are all sorts of things to be learnt as I stand at the kitchen sink.

Finding the revelation of God in the everyday does not just mean identifying allegories ('My heart was dirty until God washed it clean.'). It means having eyes to see God's active involvement in his world. It means tracing his handiwork in the everyday.

YOUR KITCHEN SINK CAN BE A HOLY PLACE

One of the common themes in missional church literature is a critique of the division between secular and sacred – the idea that some aspects of life are sacred, holy, godly while other activities are, at best, indifferent as far as our faith is concerned and, at worst, corrupt and impure, best avoided as much as possible.

We can create this division in respect to both space and time. We can create holy spaces and secular spaces. A church building is a holy place; if it is not inherently sacred then at least it is the location where holy activities take place. In other words, we may not go as far as venerating the building itself, but when we think of Christian activities or when we think of serving God, we think of activities that take place within a church building or the gathering of God's people wherever that might be. We make a distinction between holy space and secular space, if not in our articulated theology then in our practical assumptions.

Or we make a distinction between holy time and secular time. Christian activities include prayer meetings, evangelism, church services, Bible studies, personal devotions. Activities such as changing nappies, serving customers, playing football are all secular activities and therefore less holy. They may be seen as legitimate activities, but not gospel activities; not activities that are done as an outworking of the gospel. Or they may be viewed as distractions from real Christian service.

We make a distinction between holy space and secular space.

Missional theology rejects this division. Christian service is not something that takes place within church or when the church gathers or when evangelism takes place. It is not less than these things, but it is much more. Christian service takes place in day-to-day life; its occasion and location is everyday life. Indeed, the church is not a building (a space within space), nor is it an event (a time within time). The church is the community of God's people sharing life – ordinary life, everyday life – at any moment and in any place with gospel intentionality.

This reflects a radical shift in the Bible story. Under the Old Covenant there was a sacred-secular divide. They spoke of things as being clean and unclean. The book of Leviticus sets up a complete system of graduated holiness. At the centre of the tabernacle or temple was the Holy of Holies, the most holy place. Then there was the Holy Place. The further you moved from the temple, the less holy you were. And depending on who you were and what you had done or what you had touched or where you were in your menstrual cycle, you had to locate yourself within this system of graduated holiness, a series of concentric circles in which space was more holy as you moved towards the centre. Leviticus 15, for example, says:

> *The LORD said to Moses and Aaron, 'Speak to the Israelites and say to them: 'When any man has a bodily discharge, the discharge is unclean. Whether it continues flowing from his body or is blocked, it will make him unclean. This is how his discharge will bring about uncleanness . . .*
>
> *'Anyone the man with a discharge touches without rinsing his hands with water must wash his clothes and bathe with water, and he will be unclean till evening.*
>
> *'A clay pot that the man touches must be broken, and any wooden article is to be rinsed with water.*

'When a man is cleansed from his discharge, he is to count off seven days for his ceremonial cleansing; he must wash his clothes and bathe himself with fresh water, and he will be clean. On the eighth day he must take two doves or two young pigeons and come before the LORD to the entrance to the Tent of Meeting and give them to the priest. The priest is to sacrifice them, the one for a sin offering and the other for a burnt offering. In this way he will make atonement before the LORD for the man because of his discharge.' (vv. 1–3;11–15)

You were in a constant process of being defiled and being reconsecrated, negotiating your way through this geography of holiness. There was a space within space that was holy, the temple. And there was a time within time that was holy – the Sabbath. One day in seven was holy to the Lord. And this time within time demanded a different kind of behaviour, just as the temple was a space within space that required different behaviour.

> **There was a time within time that was holy – the Sabbath. One day in seven was holy to the Lord.**

The coming of the New Covenant brings an end to these distinctions. We see them disappearing in the ministry of Jesus. In Mark 1 Jesus touches a leper (vv. 40–44), a touch that under the Old Covenant law made Jesus unclean. Jesus ought to be excluded from the holy space. He can only be included again after he has been recleansed. But instead what happens when Jesus touches the leper is that the leper is cleansed and the leper is included. It is the same with the woman with an issue of blood in Mark 5:25–34. Jesus refines the geography of holiness.

We see the distinctions ebbing away when the disciples eat corn or when Jesus heals on the Sabbath day (see Matt. 12:1–14). What makes an event holy is not the day on which it takes place, but the saving activity of Jesus.

Above all, Jesus reshapes the geography of holiness at the cross. What was the point of the Levitical system of graduated holiness? What was its point when God's plan was always that the system would be abolished by the coming of Jesus? The point was to teach us the infinite holiness of God. God is not to be trifled with. Holiness matters. You cannot abolish holiness. God is a consuming fire. The Levitical system was designed to teach us the risk, the challenge, the apparent impossibility of human beings coming into the presence of a holy God. Holy space is not for us! We do not belong. It is dangerous, deadly space.

God is not to be trifled with. Holiness matters. You cannot abolish holiness. God is a consuming fire.

But when Jesus dies, the curtain of the temple is torn in two. The curtain that screened us off from the Holy of Holies is removed. Now we are welcomed into the presence of the holy God. Now we can inhabit holy space and holy time. Not because holiness no longer matters, but because Jesus sanctifies us, Jesus consecrates, Jesus makes us holy.

So now *Jesus* is the time within time and the space within space. The *Lord* of the Sabbath is here, inviting people to find rest not in a day, but in him (Matt. 11:28 – 12:14). The temple is *his* own body which is raised on the third day (John 2:18–22). It is the presence of Jesus that consecrates time and space. Holiness is located in Christ.

But Jesus is now absent. He has ascended into heaven. And he ascended bodily just as he rose bodily. This means that his location is elsewhere, in heaven. He is no longer here. So the holy space is heaven.

Heaven is the holy place. It is the place where God's will is done. It is the place where God is present.

There is more to say, but let us not jump over this statement too quickly. Heaven is the holy place. It is the place where God's will is done. It is the place where God is present. And so it relativizes all earthly claims – even, dare I say, the claims of practitioners of missional church, that all of life is holy.

Earth is not a holy place. Much of it is ugly, rebellious, a seething cauldron of evil just as Babel was. My city and your city (or town, or village) are not holy places. They are sinful places.

Heaven is also the place whence the future comes. Heaven's time is holy time. It is the place where God's future is already a reality, where God's will is already done. Meanwhile, history is not holy. Our newspapers do not chronicle holiness. History is the story of our rebellion against God and our failure to love one another.

However, the absent Christ is present with us through his Spirit, the Holy Spirit, the Spirit of holiness. The Spirit is constantly creating time within time and space within space that is holy. He inspires, energizes, and motivates holy activity, done for God and in the presence of God.

The Spirit is constantly creating time within time and space within space that is holy.

So, through the Spirit, holiness invades history and the earth. This means there is a space within space which is holy, and a history within history that is the story of holiness. But this holy space within space and this holy time within time is no longer about special times and places. The holy space and holy time are construed in a radically different way; a way that is centred on the Holy Spirit. Holy time and space are about the Spirit mediating God's holy presence as the basis of Christ's work in the midst of ordinary, everyday life. It is the new city within the old city, the new humanity within the old humanity, the new age within the old age.

Let us sharpen this up by delineating some different theological options.

1. It is no longer the case that some parts of life are sacred and some are secular, that there are holy spaces within space and there are holy times within time.

2. But neither is it the case that all of time and all of space is holy.

3. Instead the Spirit mediates the presence of Christ to create holy moments within everyday life.

The prophecy of Zechariah ends with these words:

> *On that day even the harness bells of the horses will be inscribed with these words: HOLY TO THE LORD. And the cooking pots in the Temple of the LORD will be as sacred as the basins used beside the altar. In fact, every cooking pot in Jerusalem and Judah will be holy to the LORD of Heaven's Armies. All who come to worship will be free to use any of these pots to boil their sacrifices. And on that day there will no longer be traders in the Temple of the LORD of Heaven's Armies. (Zech. 14:20,21 NLT)*

Under the Old Covenant, holiness was tied to special times

and special places. The temple was holy. Its pots were holy. To enter you had to be ritually clean. But now every pot in Judah is holy. Every pot in your kitchen is holy. Anywhere and anytime can be holy. *Your kitchen sink can be a holy place if you offer up your washing of the dishes to God as a sacrifice of praise, sharing his delight in creation and serving others in love.*

EVERYDAY MISSION

That is enough talk about washing the dishes. Some of you have dishwashers and these images may seem irrelevant to you! But what I have tried to do is illustrate how the gospel profoundly touches everyday life. I have tried to model a pattern of thinking that you can – you should – apply to every aspect of life. We should talk about these kinds of issues in our Christian communities as we share life together, so that a gospel perspective on everyday life becomes the currency of our conversation and behaviour.

The gospel does not simply belong to Sunday mornings. It is also for Monday mornings. It does not belong to a quiet time and opportunities to share the gospel.

The gospel does not simply belong to Sunday mornings. It is also for Monday mornings. It does not belong to a quiet time and opportunities to share the gospel. It affects every moment, every relationship, every activity.

This attitude may help you do mission. If you do not have an everyday gospel, then the gospel will become a formula that you have to crowbar into conversations. But an everyday gospel creates opportunities every day to talk about Jesus.